COAL MINER

BY NICK GORDON

BELLWETHER MEDIA · MINNEAPOLIS, MN

Are you ready to take it to the extreme?
Torque books thrust you into the action-packed world
of sports, vehicles, mystery, and adventure. These books
may include dirt, smoke, fire, and dangerous stunts.
WARNING: read at your own risk.

Library of Congress Cataloging-in-Publication Data

Gordon, Nick.
 Coal miner / by Nick Gordon.
   p. cm. -- (Torque: dangerous jobs)
 Includes bibliographical references and index.
 Summary: "Engaging images accompany information about coal miners. The combination of high-interest
subject matter and light text is intended for students in grades 3 through 7"--Provided by publisher.
 ISBN 978-1-60014-893-4 (hbk. : alk. paper)
 1. Coal miners--Juvenile literature. 2. Coal mines and mining--Juvenile literature. I. Title.
 HD8039.M615G67 2013
 622'.334--dc23
                                    2012039853

TABLE OF
CONTENTS

CHAPTER 1

CAVE-IN!

A group of coal miners works hundreds of feet underground. **Methane** gas slowly fills the dark mine. Boom! The methane explodes. The mine shakes as a tunnel caves in. Tons of rock crash down and thick dust fills the air. The miners are trapped!

Rescue workers race against time. They know the miners cannot survive for long. They also worry about another cave-in. The workers dig day and night. They lower food and water down an opening. Three days later, they pull the miners to safety. The miners are weak and tired. But they are alive.

CHAPTER 2

COAL MINERS

Coal provides about half of the electricity in the United States. Power plants burn it to create energy. Coal miners dig into the ground for this **natural resource**. They use explosives and heavy machinery. Collecting coal is hard, dangerous work.

coal

On the Surface

Not all coal mines are underground. Miners also dig for coal in open-air surface mines. They don't have to worry about cave-ins. Still, working with heavy machinery is always dangerous.

Coal miners need safety gear. They wear hard helmets, goggles, and gloves. Special masks keep them from breathing coal dust. Many mines also have emergency oxygen tanks. They give trapped miners air to breathe.

Dangerous Odds

On average, about 30 coal miners die on the job each year in the United States.

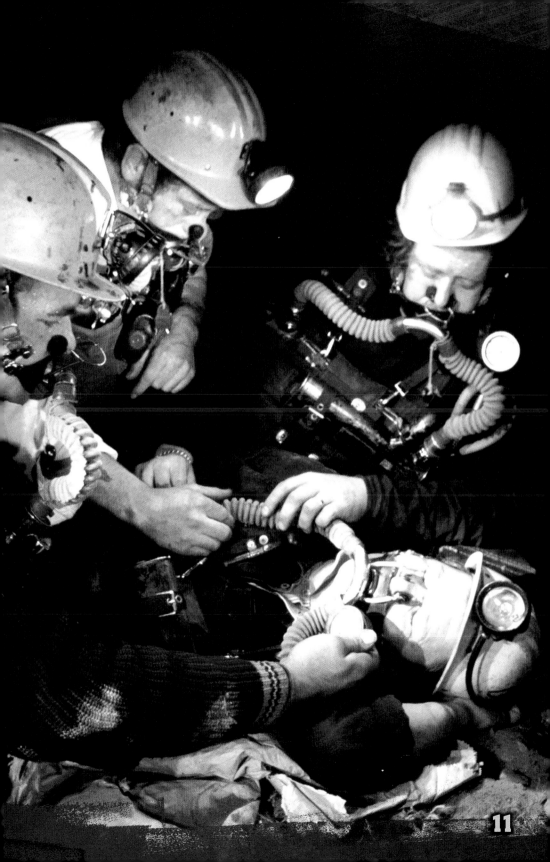

Watch the Birdie

Miners used to bring canaries into mines with them. The birds are sensitive to the buildup of gases. A dead canary was a sign that miners should leave a mine.

Coal mines are safer today than in the past. They are built with safety features. Sensors check the air quality. Advanced **ventilation** systems move air into and out of the mines. Wood **braces** help to prevent cave-ins.

braces

Miners still need to be prepared for accidents. They must know how to respond to emergencies. Sometimes they get trapped underground. They must survive while they wait to be rescued. A rescue can take days or even weeks!

The Deadliest Year

In 1907, more than 3,000 coal miners died on the job in the United States. It is the deadliest year on record.

CHAPTER 3

DANGER!

Cave-ins are one of the biggest dangers to miners. Tons of rock can **collapse** without warning. The falling rock can crush miners. It can also trap them underground. Trapped miners often die of **suffocation** or **dehydration**.

Tired Miners

Miners often work 12 hours or more a day. Tired miners make more mistakes. Some companies are making shifts shorter to improve safety.

Mines have many other dangers. Gases can build up. Some are poisonous to people. Others can explode. Fire in a mine can also be deadly. There is nowhere for the heat and smoke to escape. The same is true for water. Floods can quickly fill a mine.

Is It Damp In Here?

Miners call gas buildups "damps." A fire damp is methane. A black damp is carbon dioxide and nitrogen. A white damp is poisonous carbon monoxide.

Coal miners also face long-term threats. One is **black lung disease**. Miners breathe in a lot of coal dust. The black dust can build up in their lungs. Black lung disease affects breathing and often leads to death. It is just one more threat that comes from one of the world's most dangerous jobs.

Tragedy on the Job

In 2010, methane gas built up in a coal mine in West Virginia. The gas caused an explosion that killed 29 miners. It was the deadliest coal mining accident in the U.S. in 40 years.

Glossary

black lung disease—a deadly lung disease caused by breathing in coal dust

braces—structures that help hold up a tunnel or mine shaft

collapse—to fall suddenly

dehydration—a lack of water and body fluids

methane—an invisible gas that can easily catch fire and explode

natural resource—a substance collected from nature and used by humans

suffocation—death caused by a lack of breathable air

ventilation—the movement of air into and out of an enclosed space

To Learn More

AT THE LIBRARY

Chapman, Garry, and Gary Hodges. *Coal*. Mankato, Minn.:
Smart Apple Media, 2011.

Hyde, Natalie. *Life in a Mining Community*. New York, N.Y.:
Crabtree Pub., 2010.

Reeves, Diane Lindsey. *Scary Jobs*. New York, N.Y.: Ferguson,
2009.

ON THE WEB

Learning more about coal miners
is as easy as 1, 2, 3.

1. Go to www.factsurfer.com.

2. Enter "coal miners" into the search box.

3. Click the "Surf" button and you will see a list of
related Web sites.

With factsurfer.com, finding more information
is just a click away.

Index

The images in this book are reproduced through the courtesy of: Jan Stromme/
Getty Images, front cover, pp. 20-21; AFP/Getty Images, pp. 4-5; STR/AFP/
Getty Images/Newscom, pp. 6-7; Juan Martinez, p. 8; Cultura Limited/
SuperStock, pp. 8-9; Bob Thomas/Getty Images, pp. 10-11; Tone Koene/Age
Fotostock, pp. 12-13; Tyler Stableford, pp. 14-15; Corbis Flirt/Alamy, p. 17;
Nomad/SuperStock, p. 18; Exacto Stock/SuperStock, pp. 18-19.